W9-CQS-727

# THOUGHTS
# FOR
# A GOOD
# LIFE

DECORATED BY RUTH McCREA

THE PETER PAUPER PRESS
MOUNT VERNON · NEW YORK

# NOTE

*Because this is a time when so many are led by their cravings for easy money, easy pleasure, and easy living, it is good to be reminded that there are other ways to live, and to think about life.*

*This little collection of thoughts for a good life is therefore dedicated to those who still believe that the right way to live is by simple honesty and charity, love for one's fellow man, cheerful responsibility and work.*

# THOUGHTS
## FOR
## A GOOD
## LIFE

1st. A happy life consists in tranquility of mind.

2nd. He that can have patience can have what he will.

3rd. Kind hearts are more than coronets.

4th. If you can't help your friend with money, help him at least with a sigh.

5th. Honor the tree that gives you shelter.

6th. Being ignorant is not so much a shame, as being unwilling to learn.

7th. A joy that's shared is a joy made double.

8th. Live and let live is the rule of common justice.

9th. Knowledge is the wing wherewith we fly to heaven.

10th. That day is lost on which one has not laughed.

11th. He who lends to the poor gets his interest from God.

12th. The secret of life is not to do what you like, but to like what you do.

13th. The life of man is the plaything of Fortune.

14th. Man's love is of man's life a thing apart, but 'tis woman's whole existence.

15th. Modes and customs vary, but human nature is the same.

16th. What therefore God hath joined together, let not man put asunder.

17th. When the one man loves the one woman and the one woman loves the one man, the very angels leave heaven and come and sit in that house and sing for joy.

18th. What is taken in with the milk, only goes out with the soul.

19th. Learn to see in another's misfortune the ills which you should avoid.

20th. It is but an empty purse that is full of other men's money.

21st. God could not be everywhere and therefore he made mothers.

22nd. A good name keeps its luster in the dark.

23rd. Obedience is the mother of success, the wife of safety.

24th. Those who never retract their opinions love themselves more than they love truth.

25th. Folks who have no vices have very few virtues.

26th. Our greatest happiness does not depend on the condition of life in which chance has placed us, but is always the result of a good conscience, good health, occupation — and freedom in all just pursuits.

27th. Be of use to humanity, and you will learn to love human beings.

28th. Absence diminishes little passions and increases great ones.

29th. Amusement is the happiness of those who cannot think.

30th. The devil divides the world between atheism and superstition.

31st. Make every bargain clear and plain, that none may afterwards complain.

1st. Only at the end of a man's prosperous life dare we pronounce him happy.

2nd. Violent hatred sinks us below those we hate.

3rd. Nature, time and patience are the three great physicians.

4th. Everything has its beauty but not everyone sees it.

5th. It is no honor for an eagle to vanquish a dove.

6th. Whosoever exalteth himself shall be abashed; and he that humbleth himself shall be exalted.

7th. It is better to receive than to commit an injury.

8th. You cannot judge of the wine by the barrel.

9th. No man is the wiser for his learning.

10th. A pennyweight of love is worth a pound of law.

11th. God grants liberty only to those who love it.

12th. A long life may not be good enough, but a good life is long enough.

13th. Better a dinner of herbs where love is, than a stalled ox and hatred therewith.

14th. Loyalty is the holiest good in the human heart.

15th. He is a man who acts like a man.

16th. Marriages are made in heaven.

17th. The master should bring honor to his house, not the house to its master.

18th. It is the mind that ennobles, not the blood.

19th. What he has is no more use to the miser than what he has not.

20th. Blessed are they that have not seen, and yet have believed.

21st. A mother does not hear the music of the dance when her children cry.

22nd. Music hath charms to soothe the savage beast.

23rd. No one can rule except one who can be ruled.

24th. God's in His Heaven — all's right with the world.

25th. The future destiny of the child is always the work of the mother.

26th. Timid men prefer the calm of despotism to the boisterous sea of liberty.

27th. Let us make a new rule of life: always to try to be a little kinder than is necessary.

28th. A laugh is worth a hundred groans in any market.

_March_

1st. Nature gives all the chance for happiness — knew they but how to use it.

2nd. A man is not as easily healed as he is hurt.

3rd. Where your treasure is, there will your heart be also.

4th. Dry bread at home is better than roast meat abroad.

___

5th. An hour in the morning before breakfast is worth two all the rest of the day.

___

6th. A man without knowledge is like one that is dead.

___

7th. Sorrows remembered sweeten present joy.

___

8th. Keep your breath to cool your porridge.

___

9th. Those who really thirst for knowledge always get it.

___

10th. Where is there any book of the law so clear to each man as that written in his heart?

___

11th. Liars begin by imposing on others, and end by deceiving themselves.

___

12th. The web of our life is of mingled yarn, good and ill together.

**17**

13th. There is no fear in love; but perfect love casteth out fear.

14th. The opinion of the majority is not the final proof of what is right.

15th. A man is valued according to his own estimate of himself.

16th. Therefore shall a man leave his father and mother, and shall cleave unto his wife.

17th. Everyone is both a master and a servant.

18th. A merry man lives as long as a sad one.

19th. Mistakes occur through haste, never through doing any thing leisurely.

20th. If money be not thy servant, it will be thy master.

21st. Heard melodies are sweet, but those unheard are sweeter.

22nd. The heavens declare the glory of God, and the firmament sheweth His handiwork.

23rd. Neither give offense to others, nor take offense from them.

24th. Never tell evil of a man, if you do not know it for a certainty, and if you do know it for a certainty, then ask yourself, "Why should I tell it?"

25th. We are all ready to be savage in some cause. The difference between a good man and a bad man is the choice of the cause.

26th. Most of the shadows of this life are caused by standing in our own sunshine.

27th. The whisper of a pretty woman can be heard farther than the roar of a lion.

28th. The oriental philosophers say "What I gave, I held; what I spent, I had; what I kept, I lost."

29th. He who shoots at the sun will shoot higher than he who shoots at a tree.

30th. The infidels of one age have been the aureoled saints of the next.

31st. What is beautiful is good, and who is good will soon also be beautiful.

1st. One is never so happy or so unhappy as he thinks.

2nd. Be not a baker if your head be
of butter.

3rd. A generous heart dares to speak,
it needs no preparation.

4th. Always help the lame dog over the stile.

5th. Among men of honor a word is a bond.

6th. There is no true holiness without humility.

7th. A jest that comes too near the truth leaves a sting behind.

8th. Forbear to judge, for we are sinners all.

9th. They know enough who know how to learn.

10th. The gods have not granted to mortals laughter without tears.

11th. Never read over your letters.

12th. As a man lives, so shall he die; as a tree falls, so shall it lie.

13th. They live ill who are always beginning to live.

22

14th. If the mountain will not come to Mahomet, Mahomet must go to the mountain.

15th. No greater shame to man than inhumanity.

16th. It is the cause, not the death, that makes the martyr.

17th. It is part of the cure to wish to be cured.

18th. The mills of the gods grind slowly, but they grind exceedingly fine.

19th. Any man may make a mistake; none but a fool will persist in it.

20th. All flesh is grass, and all the goodliness thereof is as the flower of the field.

21st. If you don't scale the mountain, you can't view the plain.

22nd. Never does Nature say one thing and Wisdom another.

23

23rd. Obedience is yielded the more readily to one who commands gently.

24th. There is a tide in the affairs of men, which taken at the flood leads on to fortune.

25th. God is love; and the love of a husband and wife brings us nearer to the heart of reality, the knowledge of God, than any other experience.

26th. Where the press is free, and every man able to read, all is safe.

27th. To be happy is to have good health and a bad memory.

28th. For the sake of one good action a hundred evil ones should be forgotten.

29th. It is hard to put old heads on young shoulders.

30th. Two arrows in the quiver are better than one, and three are better still.

*May*

1st. He is happy who knows his good fortune.

2nd. Health and cheerfulness beget each other.

3rd. He that is of merry heart hath a continual feast.

4th. A happy heart is better than a full purse.

5th. Be not forgetful to entertain strangers: for thereby some have entertained angels unawares.

6th. An indolent man draws his breath but does not live.

7th. Joy is like the ague; one good day between two bad ones.

8th. Kindness is more binding than a loan.

9th. A good laugh is sunshine in a house.

10th. Laws too gentle are seldom obeyed; too severe, seldom executed.

11th. A man can become learned by asking questions.

12th. Blessed are the meek: for they shall inherit the earth.

13th. Give us grace to listen well.

14th. If you would be loved, love and be lovable.

15th. What the superior man seeks is in himself: what the small man seeks is in others.

16th. Marriage is a lottery in which men stake their liberty and women their happiness.

17th. He has a very hard heart that does not love in May.

18th. Take care of the minutes and the hours will take care of themselves.

19th. He prepares evil for himself who plots mischief for others.

20th. Monuments are superfluous: our memory will endure if our lives have deserved it.

21st. It is better to go to the house of mourning than to seek for the house of feasting.

22nd. Remember that the sky is not less blue because the blind man does not see it.

23rd. We can exist without our friends, but not without our neighbors.

24th. None is fool enough to choose war instead of peace. For in peace sons bury fathers, but in war fathers bury sons.

25th. Too much idleness fills up a man's time much more completely, and leaves him less his own master, than any sort of employment whatsoever.

26th. Nothing astonishes men so much as common sense and plain dealing.

27th. The man who insists upon seeing with perfect clearness before he decides, never decides. Accept life, and you must accept regret.

28th. That action is best which procures the greatest happiness for the greatest numbers.

29th. The old age of an eagle is better than the youth of a sparrow.

30th. A soft answer turneth away wrath: but grievous words stir up anger.

31st. That is a good book which is opened with expectation and closed with profit.

June

1st. Happiness is made to be shared.

2nd. If you have not what you like, you must like what you have.

3rd. The heart of the fool is in his mouth, but the mouth of the wise man is in his heart.

30

4th. The higher the plum-tree the riper the plum.

5th. The darkest hour is just before the dawn.

6th. It is well to lie fallow for a while.

7th. To do injustice: more disgraceful than to suffer it.

8th. They have a right to censure that have a heart to help.

9th. The sleep of a laboring man is sweet.

10th. The law blushes when children correct their parents.

11th. The most cruel lies are often told in silence.

12th. Life is a voyage that's homeward bound.

13th. Truly the light is sweet, and a pleasant thing it is for the eyes to behold the sun.

14th. One, on God's side, is a majority.

15th. A man of words and not of deeds is like a garden full of weeds.

16th. Marriage is one year of joy, another of comfort, and all the rest of content.

17th. He that is master of himself will soon be master of others.

18th. An undisturbed mind is the best salve for affliction.

19th. Misfortune does not always come to injure.

20th. All things are born of earth; all things earth takes again.

21st. Even God cannot make two mountains without a valley between them.

22nd. Where there is music there can't be mischief.

23rd. Observation, and not old age, brings wisdom.

24th. If you love the good that you see in another, make it your own.

25th. You will find poetry nowhere unless you bring some with you.

26th. The great tree attracts the big wind.

27th. Trust men and they will be true to you; treat them greatly and they will show themselves great.

28th. Absence sharpens love, presence strengthens it.

29th. Woman is a miracle of divine contradictions.

30th. None preaches better than the ant, and she says nothing.

July

1st. Idle folk have the least leisure.

2nd. A healthy body is the guest-chamber of the soul; a sick, its prison.

3rd. Every heart hath its own ache.

4th. The highest tree hath the greatest fall.

5th. In all the wedding cake, hope is the sweetest plum.

6th. An idle person is the devil's playfellow.

7th. Weeping may endure for the night, but joy cometh in the morning.

8th. Many complain of their memory, but few of their judgment.

9th. Only one good: knowledge; only one evil: ignorance.

10th. The man who does no wrong needs no law.

11th. It is better to be lied about than to lie.

12th. I would not live always: for my days are vanity.

13th. Life can only be understood backwards; but it must be lived forwards.

14th. Machinery has greatly increased the number of well-to-do idlers.

15th. Man is a noble animal, splendid in ashes, and pompous in the grave.

16th. Love is often a fruit of marriage, not a cause of it.

17th. Boldness leads a man to heaven and to hell.

18th. There are no greater sorrows than to recall, in misery, the times when we were happy.

19th. The misfortunes hardest to bear are those which never come.

20th. A rolling stone gathers no moss.

21st. Rather thy study full of books, than thy purse full of money.

22nd. Necessity can make even the timid brave.

23rd. There is nothing new but what has been forgotten.

24th. Kind words do not wear out the tongue.

25th. When a man is wrapped up in himself, he makes a pretty small package.

26th. If heaven wishes to rain, or your mother to remarry, there is no way to stop them.

27th. All human wisdom is summed up in two words: wait and hope.

28th. Abstinence is the mother of competence.

29th. The age of gold was the age when gold did not rule.

30th. Artists, like the Greek gods, are only revealed to one another.

31st. If not seemly, do it not; if not true, say it not.

**37**

1st. No happiness without holiness.

2nd. He that loses his honesty has nothing else to lose.

3rd. When the heart is on fire, some sparks fly out of the mouth.

4th. We hate whom we have injured.

5th. As long as there is life there is hope.

6th. Wise men possess ideas; most of us are possessed by them.

7th. Better lose a jest than a friend.

8th. Kindness is the sunshine in which virtue grows.

9th. Better late than never, but best never late.

10th. Learn of the mole to plough, the worm to weave.

11th. Half the truth is often a great lie.

12th. Every man's life is a fairy-tale written by God's finger.

13th. He that hath love in his breast hath spurs in his sides.

14th. Of all the paths that lead to a woman's love pity's the straightest.

15th. Men may work and think, but women feel.

16th. The society of good women is the foundation of good manners.

17th. That which is bitter to endure may be sweet to remember.

18th. Bodies without minds are as statues in the market-place.

19th. The love of money is the root of all evil.

20th. I would rather have men ask why I have no statue than why I have one.

21st. Men are what their mothers make them.

22nd. Life is short, and we have never too much time for gladdening the hearts of those who are traveling the dark journey with us. Oh, be swift to love, make haste to be kind!

23rd. Thou shalt love thy neighbor as thyself.

24th. All is for the best in this best of all possible worlds.

25th. The only way to compel men to speak good of us is to do good.

26th. The first time it is a favor; the second a rule.

27th. The more virtuous any man is, the less easily does he suspect others to be vicious.

28th. Dispense neither counsel nor salt till you are asked for it.

29th. Every king springs from a race of slaves, and every slave has had kings among his ancestors.

30th. A great artist can paint a great picture on a small canvas.

31st. When befriended, remember it; when you befriend, forget it.

**41**

*September*

1st. Happiness is a way-station between too little and too much.

2nd. Who eat their corn while yet 'tis green; at the true harvest can but glean.

3rd. Hear twice before you speak once.

4th. A man without a home is a bird without a nest.

5th. If it were not for hope, the heart would break.

6th. For the unhappy, how slowly pass the hours!

7th. No one is injured except by himself.

8th. The heart benevolent and kind, the most resembles God.

9th. Look before you leap.

10th. He that hath a trade hath an estate.

11th. Leisure is the time for doing something useful.

12th. He that lives longest lives but a little while.

13th. Today let me live well; none knows what may be tomorrow.

14th. Maidens must be mild and meek, swift to hear and slow to speak.

15th. Man that is born of woman is of few days, and full of trouble.

16th. The greatest enemy to man is man.

17th. It is good to rub and polish our minds against those of others.

18th. Those only deserve a monument who do not need one.

19th. He who cannot bear misfortune, is not worthy of good fortune.

20th. A noble mind is free to all men.

21st. Simply having children does not make mothers.

22nd. Patience is the best medicine there is for a sick man.

23rd. He loves his country best who strives to make it best.

24th. The man who never alters his opinion is like standing water, and breeds reptiles of the mind.

25th. Grant that I may not criticize my neighbor until I have walked a mile in his moccasins.

26th. If a man does not receive guests at home, he will meet very few hosts abroad.

27th. A teacher affects eternity; he can never tell where his influence stops.

28th. One can advise comfortably from a safe port.

29th. I don't know who my grandfather was; I am much more concerned to know who his grandson will be.

30th. What's the good of a fair apple, if it has a worm in its heart?

*October*

1st. Harvest comes not every day, though it comes every year.

2nd. When corn is ripe, 'tis time to reap.

3rd. He who confers a benefit on anyone loves him better than he is beloved.

4th. He is a governor that governs his passions, and he a servant that serves them.

5th. It is a worthier thing to deserve honor than to possess it.

6th. To be for one day entirely at leisure is to be for one day an immortal.

7th. True innocence is ashamed of nothing.

8th. Men judge the affairs of others better than their own.

9th. Kindness consists in loving people more than they deserve.

10th. Learning without thought is labor lost; thought without learning is dangerous.

11th. Though God take the very sun out of heaven, yet we still must have patience.

12th. Men are sleeping, and when they die, they wake.

13th. A book that is shut is but a block of wood.

14th. Of what use is learning without understanding?

15th. Ye cannot serve God and Mammon.

16th. The only thing that can hallow marriage is love.

17th. How beautiful upon the mountains are the feet of him that bringeth good tidings, that publisheth peace.

18th. An ounce of mirth is worth a pound of sorrow.

19th. True happiness springs from moderation.

20th. The morning to the mountain, the evening to the fountain.

21st. Children are the anchors that hold a mother to life.

22nd. What's in a name? that which we call a rose by any other name would smell as sweet.

23rd. A hedge between keeps friendship green.

24th. A place for everything and everything in its place.

25th. They who love are but one step from heaven.

26th. If you are standing upright, don't worry if your shadow looks crooked.

27th. That man to whom everybody allows the second place, has an undoubted title to the first.

28th. Gold is tried by fire, brave men by adversity.

29th. A wise man is never less alone than when alone.

**49**

30th. If you are poor, distinguish yourself by your virtues; if rich, by your good deeds.

31st. Beauty without virtue is a flower without perfume.

1st. A soft answer turneth away wrath.

---

2nd. A good name is rather to be chosen than great riches.

---

3rd. The heart of the wise should reflect all objects, without being sullied by any.

4th. High houses are mostly empty in the upper storey.

5th. I am myself the guardian of my honor.

6th. The day you do not sweep your house, unexpected visitors will come.

7th. Real problems can be overcome; it is only the imaginary ones that are unconquerable.

8th. He who is a judge between two friends loses one of them.

9th. Knowledge in youth is wisdom in age.

10th. The law is for the protection of the weak more than the strong.

11th. Great passions and incurable diseases: the very remedies oft make them worse.

12th. Life is a pure flame and we live by an invisible sun within us.

13th. Whether the pitcher strike the stone, or the stone the pitcher, woe to the pitcher.

14th. Magistrates are to obey as well as execute laws.

15th. Nature revolves, but mankind advances.

16th. Meat is much, but manners are more.

17th. Just scales and full measure injure no man.

18th. Preach not because you have to say something, but because you have something to say.

19th. A fool may make money, but it needs a wise man to spend it.

20th. Put not your trust in money, but put your money in trust.

21st. Who takes the child by the hand takes the mother by the heart.

22nd. The Lord prefers common looking people. That is the reason He made so many of them.

23rd. As the rolling stone gathers no moss, so the roving heart gathers no affection.

24th. Keep thou from temptation, and God will keep thee from sin.

25th. At the end of the day flattery and censure never know which has done the most harm.

26th. To understand your parents' love, you must raise children yourself.

27th. The world has so many critics because it is so much easier to criticize than to appreciate.

28th. We can no more spend all our waking hours in consciously striving toward higher things than we can dine exclusively off jam.

29th. The righteous promise little and perform much; the wicked promise much and perform not even a little.

30th. In nothing do men more nearly approach the gods than in doing good to their fellow-men.

*December*

1st. Oh, make us happy and you make us good.

2nd. The selfish heart deserves the pain it feels.

3rd. Good health and good sense are two great blessings.

4th. A holy habit concealeth not a foul soul.

5th. When a man does not know what harbor he is making for, no wind is the right wind.

6th. As well expect to grow stronger by always eating as wiser by always reading.

7th. It is heaven's will for sorrow to follow joy.

8th. Who bathes in worldly joys, swims in a world of tears.

9th. A man is rich in proportion to the number of things he can afford to let alone.

10th. Law cannot persuade where it cannot punish.

11th. The way of this world is to praise dead saints and persecute living ones.

12th. He that begins to live begins to die.

13th. Live righteously; you shall die righteously.

14th. The magic of first love is our ignorance that it can ever end.

15th. It is no wonder to see men wicked, but it is often a wonder not to see them ashamed.

16th. It is more necessary to study men than books.

17th. God who sends the wound sends the medicine.

18th. Better to remain silent and be thought a fool, than to speak out and remove all doubt.

19th. The golden rule in life is moderation in all things.

20th. The love of money and the love of learning seldom meet.

21st. Mother is the name for God in the lips and hearts of little children.

22nd. No men sleep so soundly as they that lay their heads upon old Nature's lap.

23rd. Take no offense where none is meant.

24th. Love is a short word, but it contains everything.

25th. Music is the medicine of a troubled mind.

26th. Let every man be swift to hear, slow to speak.

27th. Oaks may fall when reeds brave the storm.

28th. Nobody can give you wiser advice than yourself.

29th. A man gazing at the stars is at the mercy of every puddle on the road.

30th. A man that keeps riches and enjoys them not, is like an ass that carries gold and eats thistles.

31st. A man is not completely born until he is dead.